$\mathcal{B}$ecoming a grandparent is a second chance. For you have a chance to put to use all the things you learned the first time around and may have made a mistake on. It's all love and no discipline.

- Dr. Joyce Brothers

Great Quotations, Inc.

All rights reserved. No part
of this book may be
reproduced or
transmitted in any
form or by any
means, electronic or
mechanical, including
photocopying,
recording or by any
information storage and
retrieval system, without permission in
writing from the publisher.

Written By:
Millie Mackiney

Cover Design By:
Icon Digital Design & Illustration, Inc.,
Naperville, IL

Typography By:
Icon Digital Design & Illustration, Inc.

Published By:
Great Quotations Publishing Co.,
Glendale Heights, IL

ISBN #1-56245-419-6

Printed in Hong Kong, 2000.

This journal is for _____

My _____

Written for you by _____

Your _____

Presented to you on _____ with love.

*I love old things: weather
beaten, worn things, cracked,
broken, torn things, the old sun,
the old moon, the earth's face,
old ships and old wagons, old coin
and old lace, rare old lace.*

- Wilson Mac Donald

I was born on _August 19, 1942_ at _Waynesboro Hospital_

In _Waynesboro, Pennsylvania 17268_

My hair was _Brown_

And my eyes were _Dark Brown_

My Mother's name was _Marie Alice Tressler Harbaugh_

And my Father's name was _Earl Walter Harbaugh_

We lived at _R.D. #1, Fairfield, Pennsylvania 17320_

In _Between Zora and Fountaindale_

When I was born, there were
_____ 0 _____ other children in our family.

After my birth, these siblings
were added to our family:

Robert Earl Ellsworth Harbaugh, September 27, 1953

My earliest memory is from when
I was about _____ years old.

_____

_____

_____

_____

_____

_____

_____

_____

_____

_____

_____

_____

Family faces are
magic mirrors.
Looking at people
who belong to us,
We see the past,
present and future.

- Gail Lumet Buckley

The first birthday that I remember
was when I was _____ years old.

That memory is special because...

_____

_____

_____

_____

_____

_____

_____

_____

_____

_____

_____

_____

The first holiday that I remember is

_____ of 19 _____ .

When I was just _____ years old.

The special memory I have of that year is

_____

_____

_____

_____

_____

_____

_____

_____

_____

_____

There is a story about me when
I was little that my family always
liked to tell...

*You can't light a candle
to show others the way,
Without feeling the warmth
of that bright little ray;
And you can't give a rose
all fragrant with dew,
Without some of its sweetness
remaining with you.*

My first year in school was 19_53_

The name of my school was _Fairfield Elementary_

It was _6 miles_ from where we lived
and I got there everyday by _Bus_

The thing I remember best about my
first year in school is _I could not open my milk box and_
my friend Nancy Gladhill opened it for me -

My first crush was on Michael Reindallar.

My favorite subject in school was _Reading_

Because _I loved to read and escaped from boring times._

And my least favorite was _Math_

Because _I can not do Math!_

Some of the games we enjoyed at school were

Jump rope
Jacks
Merry go around
Old Maid card game

As I got older, I attended _Fairfield High School - I graduated_
in 1965 - 10th in my class of 54 students.

I also attended Washington County School of Nursing - I
quit & eloped October 20, 1965!!

And, _____

_____

_____

_____

_____

Sometimes, when I was a teenager, I liked to
Ride my bike
Shoot Snakes in the Creek

My favorite entertainers were

Bobby Rydell, Fabian, Bobby Vinton, Paul Anka, Annette Funicello, Roy Rogers, Dale Evans, Wild Bill Hickock, Lone Ranger, Rin Tin Tin, Johnny Horton,

My favorite songs were

Sweet Sixteen, Rose Garden, Barbara Ann, The Battle of New Orleans,

And whenever I hear them, I think of

a much slower time of life

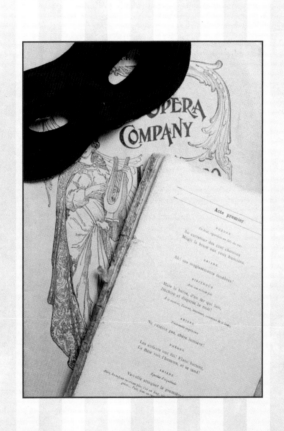

I'll never forget the time that _____
_____
_____
_____
_____
_____
_____
_____
_____
_____
_____
_____
_____
_____
_____
_____
_____

Into the woman's keeping is committed the destiny of the generations to come after them.

- Theodore Roosevelt

When I went on my first date,

I was _____ 17 _____ years old

And we went to _the Junior - Senior Prom of 1965_

I was supposed to be home by _Midnight_

But _we did not get home until 6:00 A.M.! My parents were really mad!_

My favorite radio or TV shows were

Hawdy Doody, Roy Rogers, Dale Evans, Wild Bill Hickok, Life of Riley, Beverly Hillbillies

And my favorite stars were

Roy Rogers, Dale Evans, Annie Oakley,

At home, I was supposed to help out by

Drying the Dishes,
Making My Bed,
Dusting
"Shell" Beans

In the summer, for vacations, we would

Go To Hershey Park & pack a picnic & visit their zoo!

One time went to Canton, Ohio to see cousins! I tore the crotch off my shorts!

In the winter, I liked to

Sled

Make snowmen

Had snowball fights

My favorite season of the year is

1. Fall - Beautiful Leaves
2. Spring - New Birth
3. Summer - picnics, can be outside
4. Winter - Hate It!

The best and most beautiful things in the world cannot be seen or even touched. They must be felt with the heart.

- Helen Keller

The best thing about my mother was

She was always home when I got home from school!
She was a very good cook!
She had lots of patience!
She was very fair and a quiet personality!

Life is the first gift,

Love is the second

And understanding the third.

- Marge Piercy

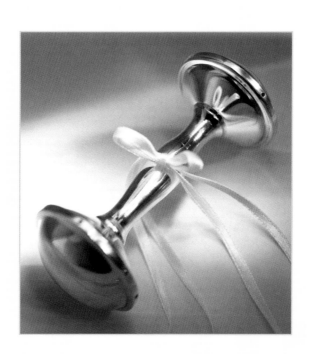

Loving a child is

a circular business;

the more you give,

the more you get,

the more you get,

the more you want

to give.

- Penelope Leach

There is so much to teach,
And the time goes so fast.
— Erma Bombeck

The best thing about my Father was

When I was young, prices were
quite different than they are now:

	Then	Now
Candy Bar	5¢	$1.00
Movie Ticket	50¢	$10.00
Soft Drink	$ 10¢	$1.50
Popcorn	5¢	$2.00
Loaf of Bread	18¢	
Gallon of Milk	92¢	
Gallon of Gas	23¢	

At family gatherings, we always
serve some special dishes.

My favorites are *Mather's Beef Barbecue*
Mother's Baked Potpie

The secret family recipe for our best dish:

_____

_____

_____

_____

_____

_____

_____

_____

_____

_____

_____

_____

_____

_____

_____

The food I have always refused to eat is

CARROTS!!

When I was younger, my favorite food was

Ham and Green Beans

But now it is

Our Family Tree

Paternal Grandfather

Walter Columbus Harbaugh

Paternal Grandmother

Lelah Wise Harbaugh

Maternal Grandfather

Elmer Ellsworth Sresler

Maternal Grandmother

Jennie Frances Sressler Sreslee

Father

Earl Walter Harbaugh

Mom

Marie Alice Sresler Harbaugh

Brothers & Sisters

Betee Florence Harbaugh Miller

Alice Harbaugh Weddle

Catherine Harbaugh Mower

Phyllis Harbaugh Lightner

Darlene Harbaugh Bricker

None - Mother was only child

My Name

Barbara Alice Harbaugh Baker

Spouse's Name

Bruce Laurence Baker, Sr.

My Children	Their Spouses
Bruce Laurence Baker, Jr.	
Brian Michael Baker	

My Grandchildren

Joshua Laurence Baker	July 16, 1992
Katheryne Anne Baker	October 26, 1993
Maddeline Rose Baker	September 8, 1998
Jared Thomas Baker	October 19, 2000

About my Children…

When I found out that I was
going to be a parent, I thought

_____

_____

_____

_____

_____

_____

_____

_____

_____

_____

_____

_____

Loving a child doesn't
Mean giving in to all
His whims; to love him
Is to bring out the
Best in him, to teach
Him to love what is difficult.

- Nadia Boulanger, Teacher

Who is getting more pleasure from this rocking, the baby or me?

- Nancy Thayer

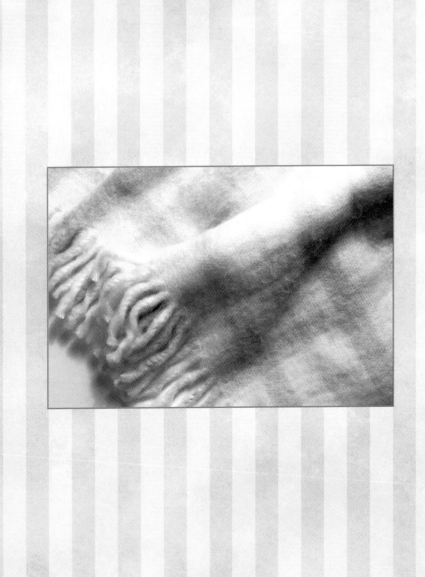

When I saw my baby for the first time,
I remember

The best thing about having a baby is

The worst thing about having a baby is

Special memories of my children and our home

To talk to a child,

to fascinate him,

Is much more difficult that

to win an electoral victory.

But it is more rewarding.

- Collette

Children are most likely to live up to what you believe of them.

*- Lady Bird Johnson,
Former First Lady*

What feeling is so nice
as a child's hand in yours?
So small, so soft and warm,
Like a kitten huddling
In the shelter of your clasp.

- Anonymous

*The walks and talks we have
with our two-year olds in
red boots have a great deal to do
with the values they will cherish
as adults.*

- Edith F. Hunter

Other fond memories...

Other fond memories...

_____

_____

_____

_____

_____

_____

_____

_____

_____

_____

_____

_____

_____

_____

_____

Other fond memories...

_____

_____

_____

_____

_____

_____

_____

_____

_____

_____

_____

_____

_____

_____

_____

_____

_____

Other fond memories...